CHANGE AND GROW

CHICK TO HEN

Acknowledgements: Cover: getty images/Patricia Doyle, getty images/Marc Henrie, gettyimages/ Dorling Kindersley, gettyimages/Vincenzo Lombardo, gettyimages/Marc Henrie. p1 gettyimages/Jane Burton, p2 gettyimages/Dorling Kindersley, p3 gettyimages/Peety Cooper, p4 gettyimages/Jane Burton, p5 gettyimages/3D4Medical.com, pp6–7 gettyimages/Jane Burton, p8 gettyimages/Michael Blann, p9 gettyimages/Steve Gorton and Tim Ridley, gettyimages/Jane Burton, p10 gettyimages/Jane Burton, p11 gettyimages/Steve Shott, p12 gettyimages/ Vincenzo Lombardo, p13 gettyimages/Dorling Kindersley, p14 getty/images/GK Hart/Vikki Hart, p15 gettyimages/Dorling Kindersley, gettyimages/Jane Burton, p16 gettyimages/Koki Iino, gettyimages/TSI Pictures, p17 gettyimages/Jane Burton, p18 gettyimages/Jane Burton, p19 gettyimages/Martin Ruegner, p20 gettyimages/Steve Gorton and Tim Ridley, gettyimages/Ove Eriksson, p21 gettyimages/Sharon Dominick, p22 gettyimages/Stockbyte, p23 gettyimages/Kevin Fitzgerald, p24 gettyimages/Peety Cooper.

First published by Parragon in 2009

Parragon
Queen Street House
4 Queen Street
Bath BA1 1HE, UK

ISBN 978-1-4075-5022-0

Printed in China

CHANGE AND GROW

CHICK TO HEN

LIVE. LEARN. DISCOVER.

Steve Parker

Bath · New York · Singapore · Hong Kong · Cologne · Delhi · Melbourne

LiFE BEGiNS

It's a warm day in springtime. The barnyard is busy with cows, pigs, tractors, and hens. Soon there will be even more hens.

The rooster has bright feathers.

Cock-a-doodle-do!

Wake-up call
The male is called a rooster. Early in the morning he crows loudly, "Cock-a-doodle-do!"
He wakes up the whole farm.

The start of life

The female is called a hen. The rooster and the hen get together and mate. Eggs inside the hen start to develop.

Ready to lay

When the mother hen is ready to lay her eggs, she finds a quiet, safe place for her nest.

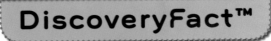

The hen's feathers are less colorful.

5

INSIDE THE EGG

The hen lays her eggs in her nest. She lays one every day or two until she has about 12. The group of eggs is known as a clutch.

Inside the egg

Each chick begins as a dark dot inside its egg. Its food is stored in the yellow yolk and the egg white, or albumin. The hard outer shell protects the growing chick.

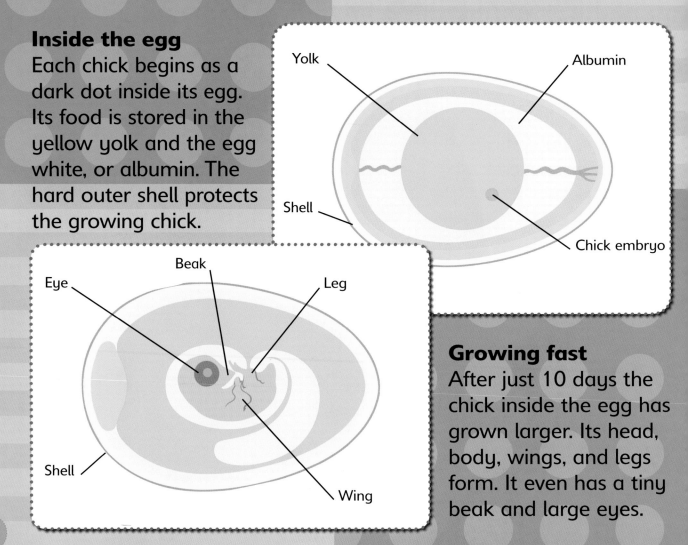

Yolk

Albumin

Shell

Chick embryo

Eye

Beak

Leg

Shell

Wing

Growing fast

After just 10 days the chick inside the egg has grown larger. Its head, body, wings, and legs form. It even has a tiny beak and large eyes.

Mom's work

The hen sits on the eggs to keep them warm. If they get too cold, the chicks inside will die.

Hatching

The hen has been sitting on, or incubating, her eggs for 20 days. Soon it will be time for the eggs to hatch.

I'm ready!
The chick starts to make cheeping noises. Its mother clucks back to encourage it.

Cheep! Cheep!

Hard work
The chick pecks a line around one end of the egg. Then it pushes off the shell with its head. This takes several hours, and the chick gets very tired.

Fluffy feathers keep the chick warm.

Growing fast

The other chicks hear the cheeping, and they start to hatch. After a day or two, all the chicks have hatched. Their wet feathers soon dry and turn fluffy and yellow.

NEW CHICK

The chick does not need to eat for the first two days. It stays close to its mother and its brothers and sisters.

Follow me!
The new chick follows the first moving thing it sees. This is usually its mother. She leads her chicks away from the nest when they are ready.

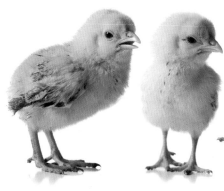

The chick has strong legs and claws.

Help! I'm lost!

Staying with Mom

The chick can see and hear well. If it gets lost it says "cheep!" and flaps its tiny wings. The mother hen will soon find it again.

Do as Mom does

The mother hen scratches and pecks on the ground for food. She sips drinks of water. The chick watches and starts to copy her.

Finding food

At first the chick pecks at everything it sees—even small pebbles and twigs. It soon learns to find grains, seeds, leaves, and other things to eat.

Help from Mom

The mother hen calls her chicks to eat. She pecks large pieces of food into smaller pieces for them to eat.

Keeping warm

The chicks rest with their mother. She may fluff her feathers over them to keep them warm.

13

LEARNING FAST

The chick is now ten days old. It can feed on its own, but it still stays close to its mother, and its brothers and sisters.

Ready to run

The chick looks and listens carefully. It is aware of the dangers all around. It can now jump and flap its wings. But its wings are small and it cannot fly yet.

Dust bath

The mother hen shows her chicks how to take a dust bath. They scratch and flap in dry soil to clean their feathers. They do not bathe in water, but drink from puddles and water troughs.

The first barnyard hens were bred thousands of years ago from red jungle fowl, which still live wild in Asia.

DiscoveryFact™

We hens get very thirsty!

TIME OF CHANGE

After a few weeks, the chick's adult feathers start to grow between its fluffy baby feathers.

Big wing feathers for flying.

Fancy feathers

The chick's wings grow big feathers for flying. It grows smaller feathers on its body to keep it dry. Under these are soft feathers called down, which keep the chick warm.

Soft down feathers to keep warm.

I am taller and slimmer.

Keeping clean

A hen uses its beak to keep its feathers clean and tidy. This is called preening.

FEATHERED FRIENDS

The chick stays with its mother, sisters, and brothers until it is about five months old. They live in a group called a flock. The chick is now a young hen or rooster.

It's good to share

The young hens and roosters like to stay near each other. If one finds some good food, the others quickly gather around to share.

A rooster has long, colorful tail feathers.

His comb is large and bright red.

He has a large, strong beak.

His wattle is large and bright red.

He is taller and heavier than the hens.

Ruling rooster
The family leader is the rooster. If another rooster arrives, he flaps, pecks, and kicks at him.

ON MY OWN

The young hens now have their adult feathers. Their wings are strong enough to fly, but hens cannot fly very well—they prefer to walk.

Out to lunch
During the day, the young hen goes off to feed around the barnyard with the other young hens. They have to look out for enemies like foxes and raccoons.

DiscoveryFact™

Homeward bound
In the evening, the hens come back to the safety of their henhouse or coop. They rest, or roost, on low perches.

Treetops
Some hens roost on the lower branches of trees.

ALL GROWN UP

The hen is now six months old. She is ready to lay her own eggs.

Eggs for eating

If the hen does not mate with a rooster, her eggs will not grow into chicks. But the eggs still have a yolk and white on the inside. The farmer collects the eggs to eat or sell.

More chicks

Soon it will be spring again and the hen will mate with the rooster. In a few months there will be more chicks following their mother around the barnyard.

Most barnyard hens live for five to ten years, but Matilda from *New Jersey* reached the grand old age of 14!

DiscoveryFact™

LiFE CYCLE

Mating
The hen and rooster mate. The eggs inside the hen's body are fertilized.

Laying
One or two days later, the hen starts to lay her eggs—she lays about one a day.

1 year
The hen is ready to mate with a rooster and have chicks of her own.

Sitting
After two weeks, all the eggs are laid. The hen sits on them to keep them warm.

6 months
The hen starts to lay eggs.

Developing
The chicks begin to grow and develop fast inside the eggs.

2 months
The young hen knows its place in the flock's "pecking order."

Hatching
About 20 days after laying, the eggs hatch. The chicks rest in the nest for two days.

6 weeks
The chick has all its adult feathers. It is now a young hen.

1 week
The chick follows its mother everywhere. It copies her and learns to eat.

3 weeks
The chick's adult feathers start to appear.

2 weeks
The chick starts to explore on its own. It goes back to its mother often to rest.